Powered by the Spirit:

Choosing Kindness and Forgiveness
in Life's Tough Moments

Self-Published by
Alisa L. Grace
Sanford, FL 32771

ISBN: 9781966129462

First Edition

Printed in the United States of America

Library of Congress Cataloging-in-Publication Data
Grace, Alisa L.

Title of the Book: Powered by the Spirit: Choosing Kindness and Forgiveness in Life's Tough Moments

Library of Congress Control Number: 2024925192

Disclaimer: The views expressed in this book are those of the author and do not necessarily reflect any organizations or individuals mentioned.

Acknowledgments: The author wishes to thank God, Her Husband (Linion), Victory Temple of God, Florida SPECS, Unity Youth Association, All About Serving You, Angels-ANJ Events, NordeVest, and Love & Create Life for their support and contributions.

Dedication:

To every teenager seeking to
navigate life's challenges with grace, strength,
and the unwavering guidance of the Holy Spirit.

A Letter to the Teenager

Hey there,

Have you ever felt lost, confused, or hurt? Like you're navigating a maze of emotions and don't know which way to turn? Yeah, we've all been there.

This book, "Powered by the Spirit," is like a compass for those tricky moments in life. It's about discovering the incredible power of the Holy Spirit – a force within you that can guide, strengthen, and help you make choices you can be proud of.

Inside these pages, you'll meet Kimiyah, Levi, Nilan, and Mason – ordinary teens facing real-life struggles with friendships, arguments, and forgiveness. You'll see how they learn to lean on the Holy Spirit for guidance and how it changes everything.

This book is your tool for:

- **Understanding the Holy Spirit:** Learn who the Holy Spirit is and how He can be your constant companion and guide.

- **Making Tough Choices:** Learn to make decisions that reflect kindness and forgiveness, even when they're hard.

- **Living a Powerful Life:** Discover how to tap into the Spirit's strength to overcome challenges and live a life full of purpose.

Get ready to dive in, explore, and discover how you can be "Powered by the Spirit."

Contents

Chapter 1:
The Fall-Out

Purpose:

To introduce the characters and set the stage for a conflict, highlighting the need for forgiveness and the Holy Spirit's guidance.

The Fall-Out

"I can't believe he said that!" Levi fumed, kicking a loose stone across the sidewalk. "Right in front of everyone, too!"

Kimiyah, his ever-patient friend, listened intently. "What exactly did Mason say, Levi? Maybe it wasn't as bad as you think."

"Oh, it was bad," Levi insisted. "We were arguing about that history project, and he basically called me dumb. Said I wouldn't know a primary source if it hit me in the face!"

The memory of Mason's dismissive laugh still stung. Levi felt a wave of humiliation wash over him, followed by a surge of anger. He had always been sensitive about his grades, and Mason's words felt like a direct attack on his intelligence.

Kimiyah gently placed a hand on Levi's arm. "I know you're upset, Levi. But maybe Mason didn't mean it the way you took it. Sometimes things come out wrong, especially when we're arguing."

Levi sighed, the anger still simmering within him. "I don't know, Kimiyah. It felt intentional. Like he was trying to put me down."

"I understand," Kimiyah said softly. "But holding onto this anger isn't going to help. Have you thought about praying about it? Asking the Holy Spirit to help you figure things out?"

Levi hesitated. He knew Kimiyah was right, but the thought of forgiving Mason felt impossible at that moment.

Scripture:

"A soft answer turns away wrath, but a
harsh word stirs up anger." Proverbs 15:1

Transformative Questions:

1. Have you ever had an argument with a friend that left you feeling hurt and angry?

   _____

   _____

   _____

   _____

2. How do you usually react when someone says or does something that upsets you?

   _____

   _____

   _____

   _____

3. Do you think it's easy or difficult to forgive someone who has hurt you? Why?

   _____

   _____

   _____

   _____

Chapter 2:
The Holy Spirit's Gentle Nudge

Purpose:

To introduce the concept of the Holy Spirit as a source of comfort, wisdom, and guidance in challenging situations.

The Holy Spirit's Gentle Nudge

Kimiyah and Levi sat in comfortable silence, the afternoon sun casting long shadows across Kimiyah's bedroom floor.

"You know," Kimiyah began thoughtfully, "I've been learning a lot about the Holy Spirit lately. He's not just some distant figure; He's actually with us all the time, guiding us and helping us make good choices."

Levi looked intrigued. "What do you mean, 'good choices'?"

"Well," Kimiyah explained, "the Holy Spirit always encourages us to choose kindness, even when we're upset. He helps us see things from other people's perspectives and reminds us to forgive, just like Jesus forgave us."

Levi shifted uncomfortably. "But forgiving Mason... that's easier said than done. I still feel so angry."

Kimiyah nodded understandingly. "I know it's hard. But the Holy Spirit can give you the strength to do it. Why don't we pray together? We can ask the Holy Spirit to help you figure out what to do."

Levi, still hesitant but willing to try, closed his eyes as Kimiyah prayed. "Holy Spirit," she whispered, "please be with Levi right now. Help him to let go of his anger and find a way to forgive Mason. Show him the path to peace and reconciliation."

As Kimiyah prayed, Levi felt a strange sense of calm wash over him. Maybe holding onto this grudge wasn't the answer. Maybe the Holy Spirit was nudging him towards something better.

Scripture:

"But the Advocate, the Holy Spirit, whom the Father will send in my name, will teach you all things and will remind you of everything I have said to you." John 14:26

Transformative Questions:

1. How do you think the Holy Spirit communicates with us?

_____

_____

_____

_____

2. Have you ever felt a "gentle nudge" guiding you towards a decision or action?

_____

_____

_____

_____

3. How can we learn to be more attentive to the Holy Spirit's guidance in our lives?

_____

_____

_____

_____

Chapter 3:
The Struggle to Forgive

Purpose:

To explore the internal struggle of choosing forgiveness, even when it feels difficult, and to emphasize the importance of empathy and understanding.

The Struggle to Forgive

Meanwhile, Mason was wrestling with his own feelings of guilt and pride. He hadn't meant to hurt Levi, but his words had come out harsher than intended. Now, he felt stuck.

"It's not like I can just go up to him and apologize," he grumbled to Nilan, their mutual friend. "He probably hates me."

Nilan, ever the peacemaker, tried to reason with him. "Come on, Mason. You guys are best friends. Just give it some time, let things cool down a bit, and then talk it out."

"Easy for you to say," Mason retorted. "You weren't the one who got insulted in front of everyone."

Nilan sighed. "Look, I know you're both feeling hurt and embarrassed. But don't let this ruin your friendship. Be the bigger person, Mason. Apologize. It's the right thing to do."

Across town, Kimiyah was having a similar conversation with Levi. "Forgiving Mason doesn't mean ignoring what happened," she explained. "It just means releasing the anger and giving him a chance to make things right."

Levi looked unconvinced. "But what if he doesn't even care?"

"Then you'll know you did the right thing," Kimiyah assured him. "Forgiveness is about freeing yourself from bitterness, not about the other person."

Scripture:

"Bear with each other and forgive one another if any of you has a grievance against someone. Forgive as the Lord forgave you." Colossians 3:13

Transformative Questions:

1. Why do you think it can be so hard to forgive someone, even if we want to?

    _____

    _____

    _____

    _____

2. How can we overcome pride and choose forgiveness, even when we feel wronged?

    _____

    _____

    _____

    _____

3. What are the benefits of forgiving others, both for ourselves and our relationships?

    _____

    _____

    _____

    _____

Chapter 4:
Facing the Moment of Truth

Purpose:

*To demonstrate the power of communication,
vulnerability, and taking responsibility
for our actions in resolving conflict.*

Facing the Moment of Truth

The next day at school, Levi felt a mix of nervousness and determination. He had prayed about it, and he knew what he had to do. He spotted Mason by his locker and took a deep breath.

"Hey, Mason," Levi said, his voice surprisingly steady. "Can we talk?"

Mason looked up, surprised. "Sure," he mumbled.

They walked to a quiet corner of the library. "Look, Mason," Levi began, "I wanted to say that what you said yesterday really hurt. It made me feel disrespected."

Mason's face flushed with guilt. "Levi, I'm so sorry. I honestly didn't mean to insult you. Things just got out of hand."

Levi nodded, feeling some of the tension ease. "I know. I probably overreacted a bit too. I shouldn't have yelled at you like that."

"No, I deserved it," Mason admitted. "I was being a jerk."

A small smile touched Levi's lips. "So, are we good?"

"Yeah," Mason said, relief flooding his face. "We're good."

Kimiyah and Nilan, who had been watching from a distance, exchanged happy glances. They knew their friends had just taken a big step towards healing their friendship.

Scripture:

"Therefore confess your sins to each other and pray for each other so that you may be healed. The prayer of a righteous person is powerful and effective." James 5:16

Transformative Questions:

1. How can honest communication help resolve conflicts and strengthen relationships?

_____

_____

_____

_____

2. Why is it important to take responsibility for our actions, even when we feel justified in our anger?

_____

_____

_____

_____

3. How can we approach difficult conversations with a spirit of humility and openness?

_____

_____

_____

_____

Chapter 5:
Strengthening Friendships through Forgiveness

Purpose:
To highlight the healing and transformative
power of forgiveness in restoring and deepening relationships.

Strengthening Friendships through Forgiveness

The weight that had been pressing down on Levi and Mason for the past few days seemed to vanish. They laughed and joked like they used to, the argument fading into a distant memory.

Later that week, the four friends gathered at Kimiyah's house, sharing pizza and laughter.

"You know," Kimiyah reflected, "this whole thing really showed me how powerful the Holy Spirit can be. If we hadn't prayed and asked for guidance, things could have turned out so differently."

Levi nodded in agreement. "I was so caught up in my anger, I couldn't see a way out. But the Holy Spirit helped me to calm down and choose forgiveness."

Nilan chimed in, "And you were both brave enough to talk it out. That's not always easy, but it's so important."

Mason smiled. "I'm just glad we're all friends again. I learned my lesson about saying hurtful things, that's for sure."

Kimiyah looked at her friends, her heart filled with gratitude. "This is what it means to be powered by the Spirit," she said. "It's about choosing kindness and forgiveness, even when it's hard. And it's about trusting that the Holy Spirit will always guide us towards what's right."

Scripture:

"Above all, love each other deeply, because love covers over a multitude of sins." 1 Peter 4:8

Transformative Questions:

1. How can forgiveness lead to stronger and more meaningful friendships?

   _____

   _____

   _____

   _____

2. What are some practical ways we can show forgiveness to others?

   _____

   _____

   _____

   _____

3. How can we create a culture of forgiveness and understanding in our relationships?

   _____

   _____

   _____

   _____

Conclusion:
Growing in Kindness, Forgiveness, and Spiritual Guidance

Purpose:

To summarize the key takeaways of the book and encourage readers to actively seek the Holy Spirit's guidance in their lives.

Growing in Kindness, Forgiveness, and Spiritual Guidance

Kimiyah, Levi, Nilan, and Mason emerged from their conflict with a deeper understanding of each other and a renewed appreciation for the power of forgiveness. They had learned that even in the toughest moments, the Holy Spirit is always there to guide them towards love, peace, and reconciliation.

As you navigate the ups and downs of your own life, remember the lessons learned by these four friends. When faced with difficult situations, turn to the Holy Spirit for guidance. Choose kindness, even when it feels challenging. Extend forgiveness, even when it hurts. And trust that the Holy Spirit will empower you to make choices that reflect love, compassion, and wisdom.

The journey of faith is a lifelong adventure filled with joys and challenges. But with the Holy Spirit as your guide, you can face any obstacle with confidence and grace. So, embrace the power within you and let the Holy Spirit lead you towards a life filled with purpose, peace, and unwavering love.

Dear Reader,

Wow! You made it to the end of "Powered by the Spirit." Pat yourself on the back! It's fantastic that you took the time to explore the Holy Spirit's incredible power and how He can work in your life.

I hope this book has been like a flashlight, illuminating the path toward kindness and forgiveness, even when things get tough. Remember Kimiyah, Levi, Mason, and Nilan? Like them, you have the strength to face any challenge with the Holy Spirit.

Let's recap those three key takeaways that can transform your life:

- **Forgiveness:** Holding onto grudges is like carrying a heavy backpack full of rocks. It weighs you down! Forgiveness is about setting those rocks down and feeling free.

- **Kindness:** Kindness is like a superpower! It can make someone's day, heal hurts, and improve the world.

- **Empowerment by the Holy Spirit:** The Holy Spirit is your constant companion, guide, and source of strength. He's always there to help you make wise choices and live a life full of purpose.

Call to action: Don't close this book and forget about it! Put these principles into practice every single day. Choose kindness, forgive freely, and lean on the Holy Spirit. You've got this!

With encouragement and blessings,

Alisa L. Grace

30-Day Challenge: Intentionally Listening to the Spirit

An Encouragement Letter Before You Start

Hey, Excellent Reader,

You're about to embark on an incredible journey – a 30-day challenge to deepen your connection with the Holy Spirit! This is your chance to tune in, listen closely, and experience the unique ways He guides and empowers you.

Each day, you'll have a small challenge, a scripture to meditate on, and a question to ponder. Don't worry; it's not about being perfect; it's about being intentional. It's about opening your heart and mind to the gentle nudges, the whispers of wisdom, and the unwavering love of the Holy Spirit.

Get ready to be amazed by how much you grow and how much closer you feel to the source of all peace and strength!

You've got this!

Day 1:

Challenge: Start your day with a simple prayer, inviting the Holy Spirit to guide your thoughts and actions.

Scripture: "But when he, the Spirit of truth, comes, he will guide you into all the truth." (John 16:13)

Transformative Question: What does being guided by the Spirit of truth mean to you?

_____

_____

_____

_____

_____

_____

_____

_____

_____

_____

_____

_____

_____

_____

_____

_____

_____

_____

_____

Day 2:

Challenge: Pay attention to your inner voice throughout the day. What is it telling you?

Scripture: "The Lord directs the steps of the godly. He delights in every detail of their lives." (Psalm 37:23)

Transformative Question: How can you become more aware of how God directs your steps?

Day 3:

Challenge: Spend some time in nature today, noticing the beauty and peace around you.

Scripture: "For since the creation of the world God's invisible qualities—his eternal power and divine nature—have been seen, being understood from what has been made, so that people are without excuse." (Romans 1:20)

Transformative Question: How does experiencing God's creation help you connect with Him?

_____

_____

_____

_____

_____

_____

_____

_____

_____

_____

_____

_____

_____

_____

_____

_____

Day 4:

Challenge: Read a chapter from Proverbs and ask the Holy Spirit to show you which verse applies to your life today.

Scripture: "For the Lord gives wisdom; from his mouth come knowledge and understanding." (Proverbs 2:6)

Transformative Question: What wisdom is the Holy Spirit speaking to you today?

_____

_____

_____

_____

_____

_____

_____

_____

_____

_____

_____

_____

_____

_____

_____

_____

_____

Day 5:

Challenge: Do something kind for someone else without expecting anything in return.

Scripture: "Each of you should use whatever gift you have received to serve others, as faithful stewards of God's grace in its various forms." (1 Peter 4:10)

Transformative Question: How does serving others help you grow spiritually?

_____

_____

_____

_____

_____

_____

_____

_____

_____

_____

_____

_____

_____

_____

_____

_____

Day 6:

Challenge: Reflect on a time when you felt the Holy Spirit's presence strongly. What were the circumstances?

Scripture: "And I will ask the Father, and he will give you another advocate to help you and be with you forever— the Spirit of truth." (John 14:16-17)

Transformative Question: How does knowing the Holy Spirit is always with you bring you comfort?

_____

_____

_____

_____

_____

_____

_____

_____

_____

_____

_____

_____

_____

_____

_____

_____

_____

Day 7:

Challenge: Spend some time in silence and solitude, listening for the still, small voice of the Spirit.

Scripture: "Be still, and know that I am God." (Psalm 46:10)

Transformative Question: What distractions prevent you from hearing God's voice clearly?

_____

_____

_____

_____

_____

_____

_____

_____

_____

_____

_____

_____

_____

_____

_____

_____

_____

_____

Day 8:

Challenge: Express gratitude to God for the ways He has worked in your life.

Scripture: "Give thanks in all circumstances; for this is the will of God in Christ Jesus for you." (1 Thessalonians 5:18)

Transformative Question: What are you most thankful for today?

_____
_____
_____
_____
_____
_____
_____
_____
_____
_____
_____
_____
_____
_____
_____
_____
_____
_____
_____

Day 9:

Challenge: Forgive someone who has hurt you.

Scripture: "Bear with each other and forgive one another if any of you has a grievance against someone. Forgive as the Lord forgave you." (Colossians 3:13)

Transformative Question: How does forgiveness free you?

_____

_____

_____

_____

_____

_____

_____

_____

_____

_____

_____

_____

_____

_____

_____

_____

_____

Day 10:

Challenge: Spend time with other believers, sharing your faith and encouraging others.

Scripture: "And let us consider how we may spur one another on toward love and good deeds, not giving up meeting together, as some are in the habit of doing, but encouraging one another—and all the more as you see the Day approaching." (Hebrews 10:24-25)

Transformative Question: How does connecting with other Christians strengthen your faith?

_____

_____

_____

_____

_____

_____

_____

_____

_____

_____

_____

_____

_____

_____

_____

Day 11:

Challenge: Read a story in the Gospels and imagine yourself in the scene. How would you have felt?

Scripture: "For the word of God is alive and active. Sharper than any double-edged sword, it penetrates even to dividing soul and spirit, joints and marrow; it judges the thoughts and attitudes of the heart." (Hebrews 4:12)

Transformative Question: What does this Bible story teach you about Jesus and His character?

Day 12:

Challenge: Identify one area of your life where you need the Holy Spirit's guidance. Pray specifically about that area.

Scripture: "If any of you lacks wisdom, you should ask God, who gives generously to all without finding fault, and it will be given to you." (James 1:5)

Transformative Question: What are you asking God for wisdom about?

_____

_____

_____

_____

_____

_____

_____

_____

_____

_____

_____

_____

_____

_____

_____

_____

_____

Day 13:

Challenge: Listen to worship music that focuses on the Holy Spirit.

Scripture: "Speak to one another with psalms, hymns and spiritual songs. Sing and make music in your heart to the Lord, always giving thanks to God the Father for everything, in the name of our Lord Jesus Christ." (Ephesians 5:19-20)

Transformative Question: How does music help you connect with the Holy Spirit?

Day 14:

Challenge: Share your faith with someone today.

Scripture: "But in your hearts revere Christ as Lord. Always be prepared to answer everyone who asks you to give the reason for the hope that you have. But do this with gentleness and respect." (1 Peter 3:15)

Transformative Question: How can you be a better witness for Christ?

_____

_____

_____

_____

_____

_____

_____

_____

_____

_____

_____

_____

_____

_____

_____

_____

_____

_____

Day 15:

Challenge: Take a walk and pray, thanking God for the beauty around you.

Scripture: "I lift up my eyes to the mountains— where does my help come from? My help comes from the Lord, the Maker of heaven and earth." (Psalm 121:1-2)

Transformative Question: How does spending time in nature refresh your spirit?

_____

_____

_____

_____

_____

_____

_____

_____

_____

_____

_____

_____

_____

_____

_____

_____

Halfway There!
Letter of Encouragement

Hey again!

You're halfway through the challenge! How's it going? Are you feeling more connected to the Holy Spirit? I bet you are!

Keep up the fantastic work! Remember, this is about progress, not perfection. Every time you tune in and listen to that still, small voice, you grow and deepen your relationship with the Spirit.

Don't give up! You're doing great!

Day 16:

Challenge: Memorize a verse about the Holy Spirit.

Scripture: "And you also were included in Christ when you heard the message of truth, the gospel of your salvation. When you believed, you were marked in him with a seal, the promised Holy Spirit, who is a deposit guaranteeing our inheritance until the redemption of those who are God's possession—to the praise of his glory." (Ephesians 1:13-14)

Transformative Question: Why is it important to memorize Scripture?

_____

_____

_____

_____

_____

_____

_____

_____

_____

_____

_____

_____

_____

_____

Day 17:

Challenge: Fast from something (food, social media, etc.) for a period of time and dedicate that time to prayer and reflection.

Scripture: "But when you fast, put oil on your head and wash your face, so that it will not be obvious to others that you are fasting, but only to your Father, who is unseen; and your Father, who sees what is done in secret, will reward you." (Matthew 6:17-18)

Transformative Question: How does fasting increase your spiritual focus?

_____

_____

_____

_____

_____

_____

_____

_____

_____

_____

_____

_____

_____

_____

_____

Day 18:

Challenge: Read a passage from the book of Acts and notice how the Holy Spirit empowered the early church.

Scripture: "But you will receive power when the Holy Spirit comes on you, and you will be my witnesses in Jerusalem, and in all Judea and Samaria, and to the ends of the earth." (Acts 1:8)

Transformative Question: How does the Holy Spirit empower you to be a witness for Christ?

_____

_____

_____

_____

_____

_____

_____

_____

_____

_____

_____

_____

_____

_____

_____

_____

_____

Day 19:

Challenge: Confess any sin or weakness to God and ask for His forgiveness and strength.

Scripture: "If we confess our sins, he is faithful and just and will forgive us our sins and purify us from all unrighteousness." (1 John 1:9)

Transformative Question: What do you need to confess to God today?

_____

_____

_____

_____

_____

_____

_____

_____

_____

_____

_____

_____

_____

_____

_____

_____

_____

_____

_____

_____

Day 20:

Challenge: Spend time praying for others.

Scripture: "Therefore confess your sins to each other and pray for each other so that you may be healed. The prayer of a righteous person is powerful and effective." (James 5:16)

Transformative Question: Who are you praying for today?

_____

_____

_____

_____

_____

_____

_____

_____

_____

_____

_____

_____

_____

_____

_____

_____

_____

_____

Day 21:

Challenge: Read a Psalm and reflect on how it expresses your emotions today.

Scripture: "My soul finds rest in God alone; my salvation comes from him." (Psalm 62:1)

Transformative Question: How do the Psalms help you connect with God on an emotional level?

_____

_____

_____

_____

_____

_____

_____

_____

_____

_____

_____

_____

_____

_____

_____

_____

_____

_____

_____

Day 22:

Challenge: Do something creative that helps you express your faith (write a poem, paint a picture, compose a song, etc.).

Scripture: "Whatever you do, work at it with all your heart, as working for the Lord, not for human masters." (Colossians 3:23)

Transformative Question: How can you use your talents and creativity to glorify God?

_____

_____

_____

_____

_____

_____

_____

_____

_____

_____

_____

_____

_____

_____

_____

_____

_____

Day 23:

Challenge: Spend time with a family member and share how God works in your life.

Scripture: "Honor your father and your mother, so that you may live long in the land the Lord your God is giving you." (Exodus 20:12)

Transformative Question: How can you strengthen your relationships with your family members?

_____

_____

_____

_____

_____

_____

_____

_____

_____

_____

_____

_____

_____

_____

_____

_____

_____

Day 24:

Challenge: Unplug from all electronics for a set period of time and focus on being present in the moment.

Scripture: "Be still, and know that I am God; I will be exalted among the nations, I will be exalted in the earth." (Psalm 46:10)

Transformative Question: How does unplugging from technology impact your spiritual life?

_____

_____

_____

_____

_____

_____

_____

_____

_____

_____

_____

_____

_____

_____

_____

_____

_____

_____

Day 25:

Challenge: Reach out to someone lonely or hurting and encourage them.

Scripture: "Carry each other's burdens, and in this way you will fulfill the law of Christ." (Galatians 6:2)

Transformative Question: How can you be a source of comfort and support to others?

_____

_____

_____

_____

_____

_____

_____

_____

_____

_____

_____

_____

_____

_____

_____

_____

_____

_____

_____

Day 26:

Challenge: Reflect on the ways you have grown spiritually during this challenge.

Scripture: "But the fruit of the Spirit is love, joy, peace, forbearance, kindness, goodness, faithfulness, gentleness and self-control. Against such things there is no law." (Galatians 5:22-23)

Transformative Question: What fruit of the Spirit are you seeing in your life?

_____

_____

_____

_____

_____

_____

_____

_____

_____

_____

_____

_____

_____

_____

_____

_____

_____

Day 27:

Challenge: Write a letter to your future self, outlining your spiritual goals and how you plan to continue growing in your faith.

Scripture: "For I know the plans I have for you," declares the Lord, "plans to prosper you and not to harm you, plans to give you hope and a future." (Jeremiah 29:11)

Transformative Question: What are your spiritual goals for the future?

Day 28:

Challenge: Share a testimony of how God has worked in your life with someone else.

Scripture: "But you will receive power when the Holy Spirit comes on you; you will be my witnesses in Jerusalem, and in all Judea and Samaria, and to the ends of the earth." (Acts 1:8)

Transformative Question: How can you be a more effective witness for Christ?

_____

_____

_____

_____

_____

_____

_____

_____

_____

_____

_____

_____

_____

_____

_____

_____

Day 29:

Challenge: Spend time in prayer, thanking God for His guidance and presence throughout this challenge.

Scripture: "Do not be anxious about anything, but in every situation, by prayer and petition, with thanksgiving, present your requests to God." (Philippians 4:6)

Transformative Question: What have you learned about prayer during this challenge?

_____

_____

_____

_____

_____

_____

_____

_____

_____

_____

_____

_____

_____

_____

_____

_____

Day 30:

Challenge: Commit to continuing to listen to the Holy Spirit in your daily life intentionally.

Scripture: "And my God will meet all your needs according to the riches of his glory in Christ Jesus." (Philippians 4:19)

Transformative Question: How will you continue to seek the Holy Spirit's guidance in your life?

_____

_____

_____

_____

_____

_____

_____

_____

_____

_____

_____

_____

_____

_____

_____

_____

_____

_____

_____

_____

_____

You Did It: Congratulations!

Way to go! You completed the 30-Day Challenge! I'm so proud of your dedication and your willingness to grow closer to the Holy Spirit.

Remember, this is just the beginning! Keep seeking His guidance, keep choosing kindness, and keep forgiving freely. The adventure of faith is a lifelong journey, and the Holy Spirit will be with you every step of the way.

Keep the Momentum Going!

Here are some additional resources to help you continue your spiritual growth:

Books:

>   **The Case for Christ** by Lee Strobel
>
>   **Mere Christianity** by C.S. Lewis
>
>   **Crazy Love** by Francis Chan
>
>   **The Purpose Driven Life** by Rick Warren
>
>   **Seeking Allah, Finding Jesus** by Nabeel Qureshi

Remember:

>   **Stay connected to a community of believers.**
>
>   **Continue to read and study the Bible.**
>
>   **Make prayer a regular part of your life.**
>
>   **Serve others and share your faith.**

The Holy Spirit is with you always!

www.ingramcontent.com/pod-product-compliance
Lightning Source LLC
LaVergne TN
LVHW051430080426
835508LV00022B/3328